Asleep in Mendocino

Asleep in Mendocino

John Oswald

Copyright © 2019, John Joseph Oswald

All rights reserved. No part of this book shall be reproduced in any form, except in inclusion of brief quotation in review or with explicit written permission from the author.

ISBN: 978-0-9891863-1-5 (sc)

ISBN: 978-0-9891863-2-2 (e)

ISBN: 978-0-9891863-3-9 (a)

Thanks:

To my folks, for their toil and sweat
They bore my yokes, and they own my debt...

To the Swan
Who gave me a big bottle of ink

To Mr. Tim, my sponsor
Who snatched me out of the jaws of death
While I was bent on snatching defeat out of the jaws of victory

To Luisa, my lioness on an alien shore
For inspiring me to be and do my best, and encouraging me to publish this book

And to my Higher Power
Who gave me my pen

Preface

I am a professional writer. But my day job is left brain work – technical, precise, dry. I've dreamt of setting my right brain free on paper. There are words waiting in line. They've been piling up over the years. Some have gushed out in waves; many are years old, still waiting for liberation. New ones line up often.

This collection is the beginning – some of the first few poems I ever wrote.

Later writings - deeper, funnier, lighter, darker, more irreverent, will be published in a different book in the near future. And there are more to come.

But this stuff...This is where the ink started to flow, and I discovered writing as art and catharsis, something that didn't feel like work. It just happened when I felt something – love, loss, fear, awe, anxiety, anger, desire, hope, joy, or desperation. Putting it on paper eased the pain, or put the cherry on top.

Mendocino, California is at the heart of my favorite place on earth. Many of these poems were born in Mendocino County or about places and experiences therein. I lived and worked there on a fishing boat in the late 1980s. As I relish the memories and dream of visiting again before I set sail for new dimensions, I find myself, in many ways, and often, asleep in Mendocino.

The themes presented: Thoughts, Feelings, Dreams, and Growing Pains, are four of the ever-present realities we all deal with. Sometimes they are bright, and sometimes they are very dark. Humor can also be bright and dark, and my contributions in that realm will be published soon.

I associate almost everything with music. Some good musical pairings for these scribbles would be:

Thoughts: Kitaro–Estrella, Rush–Different Strings

Feelings: Laura Sullivan–Claire de Lune, 10cc–I'm Not in Love

Dreams: Steven Halpern–Earthrise, Pink Floyd–Echoes

Growing Pains: Creed–Who's Got My Back, Robert Plant–Big Log

The Rabbit and the Puppy is a true story. It happened on Christmas, 1988, deep in the Navarro crazy money hills. I debated whether to include it, but a dear friend knew the metaphor all too well. So with crossed fingers I'm leaving it in.

Since writing these poems, I have experienced significant healing and discovery, which will be reflected in yet another collection.

Part of my recovery has been learning to take the clothes off my heart. This book is a step in that direction. So turn the pages and take a peek.

Contents

Thoughts 1

- WORDS 2
- POETRY IS 4
- ACADEMIAC 5
- LESSONS 6
- INTEGRITY 7
- PEACE 8
- WRITER'S BLOCK 9
- FORGET 10
- DRUNKEN SCRAWL 12
- PARALLAX 14
- THE BENDS 17

Feelings 21

- COMMON GROUND 22
- WHAT'S THE BEST KISS? 29
- IT CAN'T BE OVER! 30
- FESTI (A TRAGIC COMEDY) 32
- LITTLE TREE 34
- THE RABBIT AND THE PUPPY 35
- THORNS 38
- COLD AND BLUE 40
- POISON NAIVETÉ 42
- LOVE CHOICE 44

Point Delgada 46

Dreams 49

Howl 50
Señoritas De Consuelo 52
Coconut Head 54
Freedom 56
Seadream 58
Goodnight 62
The Salt Stream 65
Laser 68
Flooded 70
Westport Wind 72
Sailors' Eyes 74

Growing Pains 77

A Man Now 78
To Be or Not to Be 80
The Brook 82
Lost 85
Memories 86
Broken Anchor 88
Cat in Cage 90
Junk House Blues 91
Bye 94
King Arthur 96
The River 100

About the Author 102

Thoughts

Words

How limited, yet glorified are we

By words

But how can I limit myself to think

That we are glorified by words?

I am limited by my sadness

In passing, not only the sadness of this

But by my sadness complete

To know that what I hold so dear

Is but an illusion

A past too soon to come

To know realities are like birds

They fly and they die and are limited

Like words

I am limited by my madness

To think that my reality

Of ignorance and bliss

Is not madness replete

Poetry Is

A simple mind's effort to be profound

A scared soul's laugh at ghosts unknown

A literary euphoria...

A man's love song with a graceful sound

For tender speech his pride's outgrown

His deepest feelings at once to impart

A time to choose words

Before rational mind

Betrays romantic heart

Academiac

There once was a dog named spot

Who labored over every thought

To the point his poor head caught on fire

While grinding in a cognitive quagmire

For the eternal words, "See Spot run"

Inspired such an explosion of rhetorical brilliance

That his spastic mind, lacking structural resilience

Did quite suddenly expire

Lessons

Lessons learned are dollars lost

We wish that they were dollars earned

But tuition is the greater cost

When the ship of fate is helplessly tossed

As the precious wheel is carelessly turned

And seas are made unnavigable, future and past

As vital charts are torn and burned

Integrity

Reality has its price

Idealism is a vice

Romanticism has its place

As justice and grace embrace

Woe to the man who forfeits sanctity

And bows to sacrilege

How wretched the man who forsakes chastity

And pawns his heritage

Integrity slips away

In the most gentle breeze

The quest to bring it home is as hopeless

In the frothy drink of hurricane gales

As the drowning man's pleas

Peace

I wish I had a peace

A peace of mind?

Heart?

No, a peace of ass

Where does my mind go when it has no use?

Morale caked with the mud

Of some asshole's hollow authority

I wish I could create

I'd do anything to feel what I'd like

But my heart is a peace of glass

This shit is oppressing

Regressing

Depressing

Repressing

Etc...

Writer's Block

Words like turds in a constipated flunky

Loads like toads in a frustrated monkey

Tears like years in the eyes of a sailor

Muffled voices chatter through the window of a trailer

Signs and times of miles to come

Rhymes and dimes jumping off a drum

Melody trickles down the mainstream of thought

Otters totter and frolic before they're caught

Is it all on the wing?

I wish so

I think not

Forget

As I lie with my head

At the foot of my bed

And the sun through the trees

As they dance in the breeze

Is a feather changing size

That tickles my resting eyes

Through the slit between the curtains

As the clouds saunter by

I see in my pain

That my caring is insane

And my worries are all vain

And I would much rather cry

Than be dead

I would much prefer to live

Than to die

The room is now dark and cool

A big cloud now in rule

And my resting eyes relax

And forget

Drunken Scrawl

Sailors reefing cotton expanse

Captain screaming

Bunch the jib

Roll up the spinnaker

Drop the spin

Spike up the jib

Drop the spin

Break out the pen

Jim can go to bed

Relax his word

Sorry to lose a legend

But the tune must live on

So lay her down on the turntable

Let her roll

Jim Croce will live forever

Let him hang upon a lover's cross

He jumped too far beyond the human crash kind of thing
Jim was creative beyond his own creativeness
And fucked himself with his addiction
To music and cocaine
But I respect him for what he did
And what he didn't do too

Parallax

Jack and Jill went up the hill

To join themselves forever

But on the way they did fall prey

To the reality known as never

They came upon a brilliant stone

Like a glorious ray of the sun it shone

From the lovely brook wherein it lay

The surprise was so sweet

Their eyes did not meet

As they ran hand in hand

Their new treasure to greet

Silent they gazed at this unequalled prize

And neither one moved as its glory filled their eyes

After some time Jack ventured forth

With the whisper, "What is it?

A diamond from the South,

Or a pearl from the North? And how did it get

   here?

It seems quite divine."

Jill replied with a wonderful sigh,

"It is the most beautiful blue

That has ever filled these eyes of mine.

How about thine?"

"Your words are not true, this gem is not blue, but

The most radiant green mine eyes have ever seen."

They discovered the stone

Changed the color it shone

With the angle at which its reflection was thrown

They could not as one perceive this display

No matter how close together were they

Arm in arm, they pressed, cheek to cheek

And leaned out over the gurgling creek

A longed-for oneness of perception to seek
But the unity of sense they could not repair
Even the smallest distance did surely impair
What was this orb which stole their security?
Was it a trinket from heaven too perfect to understand?
Or a less pleasant messenger, a bearer of harsh reality?
It seemed to this pair a thing quite unfair
But none can escape this parallax error

The Bends

Wind now calm

Waves now rest

Silence, a balm

Soothes my aching breast

Though tempted by fear

Clouded by tears

Vision is never more clear

Foresight shunned by careless smiles

Hindsight sees for many miles

Why does it seem I must always take a bow?

Why does anxiety so often crease my brow?

I never seem to be enough

To make her happy

To call her bluff

I'm so afraid to let her in

To see my fear

To see my sin

With bolted doors

Love will never last

My fear to try

Makes it hard to win

Why does apology seem an escape

My pride and identity only to rape?

Fear of defeat surrounds me with walls

To be locked away in lonely halls

Is lonely indeed

And to miss love's grand landscape

Is fear to hurt another a noble intention?

Or is it a selfish dread of loss of attention?

Bitter is rejection

Sweet is approval

Fear of the first

Brings temptation of removal

To speak truth now saves pain in the end

Be true to yourself

Be true to a friend

An honest relationship will not die

Only change

It will not break

Only bend

Feelings

Common Ground

Gliding out across the glass

She leaves her nest

In the tall still grass

High above at the break of dawn

His eyes are drawn

And his heart is lost

To the graceful swan

Little does he know...

Though taken by her is he so

That in his talons he takes a rose

And on its descent it brushes her nose

Taking the gift in her gentle beak

A slight hint of blush warms her downy cheek

As she looks to the sky and is met with a cry

His greeting, shrill but meek

Little does she know...

Her thoughts are as his though

Could such an unlikely pair

Fuse water and air?

A blazing fire is the western sky

For the day has grown old

And evening is nigh

The swan settles down for a quiet night of rest
The eagle alights on a branch by her nest
With tired wings and ruffled crest

She welcomes his gift of a fish from the sea
For her day's meals were sparse
And "Thank you," says she

His only wish to have her by his side
His feelings take flight, too strong to hide
"Fly away with me, to the blustery heights
Where my nest keeps me warm on stormy, cold nights!"

"But I cannot fly,"

Is her gracious reply

And she smiles on him softly

With a tear in her eye

"But you will learn well!"

"Swim away with me across my blue mirror

We will see our reflections, eternal and clear."

"But I have never swam

Save to dip my claws

Into the icy shallows

To obey survival's laws."

Little do they know...

Though both wish it so

Aflight or afloat

They may never both go

For many long days they ponder their plight

And neither will surrender without a great fight

They know it takes time for difference to rhyme

But both are poetic

And both very strong

And with Love as their guide

They cannot go wrong

They may never soar the blustery heights

Content in his nest on stormy, cold nights

They may never swim across her blue mirror

No matter how so to him she is dear

But one thing they know

God's grace does abound

And they will see eye to eye

When they find common ground

One quiet day while flying by

He thinks to himself, wondering

'Why does nature part us, you and I'?

Be strong swan

Don't shed a tear

They only cloud your eyes

And make vision more unclear

Be strong eagle

Don't you cry

She'll one day know

That swans can fly

What's the Best Kiss?

The one in which the hearts

Behind the lips that touch

Beat as one

The one where you have no doubt

The feeling is mutual

The one where tears of joy, love

Or even pain

Tickle the cheeks caressing each other

It Can't Be Over!

Yes, it is

Take your bow

Though you wonder how

Life goes on

It's time to learn

And yearn

And burn

And to absorb hurtful words

And looks

And goodbyes

It's time to feel

And hurt

And talk

Not with your mouth

Or hands

But your eyes

You must love now

Or be captive forever

To the pain and uncertainty

Of loss carelessly dealt with

Festi (a tragic comedy)

Touch the sky

It gets you high

When you fly

Don't look down

You'll see the ground

That you will meet

When the wind does die

Don't leave port in swells that hide the land

Don't build your house on soft and shifting sand

Don't ask why

Or be appalled

When your fortress falls

Let feelings rise

But be advised

You'll be no sooner mesmerized

Than absolutely pulverized

When identity is gone

One question only stands

When you fall into a woman's arms

Why must you fall into her hands?

Your heart's freedom lost

To one who doesn't see

Deep inside your armored shell

The sensitivity

Little Tree

I long to take my rest

To heal my tattered crest

To be lulled by your sighing branches

And there to build my nest

My weary heart longs

For your leaves' soft songs

Your delightful fruit

To you to belong

Are you too young to bear my weight?

Or will you support another? Am I too late?

Do I have rivals your refuge to seek?

Do I challenge them all, or shall I be meek?

Until I discover you

Free will I fly

And when at last I find you

I will not pass by

The Rabbit and the Puppy

I hate like hell

This little tale to tell

But I guess I'd just as well

There was once a rusty bunny buck

Who was so desperate for something to fuck

That he tried to violate an innocent little schmuck

A puppy, no less

A little baby puppy

The goat-like beast was constrained

By a concealed length of chain

But guarded was he not by rationale or decent rein

The playful little pup saw a fuzzy little friend

And trotted within reach of this carnal little fiend

The rabbit sprung upon its innocent bundle of pleasure

And encircled her with chain as a cunning means of seizure
It scared the poor pup nearly to death
As it humped the crying whelp like a junkie on meth
And a boot in its side stole its heavy breath
The owners laughed, both red in the face
Though funny to some, it's an utter disgrace
To think that rational beings would imitate this beast
In murdering a spirit, a scarring at least
It's sickening to think this world has become
A shelter for evil
An elitist, chaotic, pacifist slum
Character today is a part in a play
And rationale itself is fading away
Sadder still than the reality of the crime

Is the pathetic tolerance in this day and time
Of an evil beyond woman's deepest fears
A putrid spring that feeds an ocean of tears
And the ironic restraint placed on rational beings
Who shudder and wretch at the thought of such things
And would protect the young, the innocent, and good
Would protect the worthy, if only they could
In days of old justice was served
By men of faith, by men of iron nerve
By fatal fist or rope or gun
In an age of "civilization," nothing is done
This question I ask:
Which is barbaric, to let the barbarian run free
Or to crush the barbarian from our needless misery?

Thorns

You are the rose garden

You are the poppy

You are the forbidden fruit

Of the Garden of Eden

You are the bittersweet

You are the one

You are the serpent

So smooth and warm

You are the needle in my arm

So life-giving

Yet so deadly

So distant

And ever friendly

I knew you

I clenched your thorns

My blood warmed you

Your nectar warmed me

Our lives entwined - with no wall to cling to

A parasitic quasi-religious addiction

A desperate perfumed animal attraction

You moan and I roam in

A shower of pheromones and hormones

But

Our minds truly embrace

Cold and Blue

My hands are like gloves

Made to fit yours

And fight off the frostbite

Of silent wars

My lips are blue

When away from you

Cold and lifeless

Cold and blue

My heart sings

A sad little song

'To you I belong, to you I belong'

My spirit aches

To know yours

Like our minds

And hands

And lips

Know each other

I can't stand to think of permanent

Distance

It makes me tremble

So cold and blue

My dear

I'm just not happy

Without you

Poison Naiveté

I hold within my hand

A stone of exquisite warmth

And smoothness

And beauty

It fits my palm

Like the surest ancient truth

Eases my mind

And doubts are impossible

The soothing heat

Which whispers up my arm

Like smoke past a lamp

Wears a black hood

I am beginning to see

Flashing by

In the corner of my heart

And wields a dull knife

I am beginning to feel

Sever my skin

In the corner of my eye

And the water is tears again

The warmth of the stone

Eats the marrow in my bones

And confuses the very essence of my being

I say to the stone

"You are beauty unknown."

And the echo that I hear

Brings the distance that I fear

"With blind eyes you are seeing."

And she closes the door

Without expression

The knife sears through

And I am alone

Love Choice

So afraid of life

Every velvet ribbon

A rusty jagged chain

Drinks of naked life

My wanderlust have slain

Now the cloven path ahead

Which shall I defend?

My priceless fragile wheel

Or the fragrant living bed?

My bloody salt fed fight

Or the warmth of healing night?

My tempest without warning

Or the fragrance of the morning?

Not only flesh

Does my life's blood miss

Not only touch

Or warmth, or kiss

But why must this

Tie my heart

In such fists?

Lessons I must learn

Deeply they must burn

For a soul mate I do yearn

For the stormy gray

The lullaby green

I do yearn

Point Delgada

Pale stretch of shore

When will I see thee?

We've exchanged so many kisses

Spent each other's time

Explored each other's hearts

And painted many a rhyme

Why oh silken reach I adore

Must I farewell bid thee?

We've tasted fruits delicious

Played so many a mime

And now we must part

For all the tale of time

My thoughts to you I've poured

Countless times we've agreed

And laughed a thousand blisses

Crossed each other's lines

Without blush or alarm

But pure peace and life

To you beloved shore

Farewell do I bid thee

As I kneel at your side

And leave you with three kisses

One for every rhyme

One to seal our hearts

And one for all of time

Dreams

Howl

Let me howl above the roar

Let me roar above the howl

Through comber and fury

Let my spirit soar

As graceful as a breeze

As strong as the northwest seas

O'er heads of men of line and trawl

Past the reach of sloop and yawl

To tip the mesh and green glass ball

Of ghost clipper ships

With swollen veins

And pursed, battered lips

And roll on weathered sawbucks adrift

Let me rest in the crook of Poseidon's trident

And dive to escape his thunderous scorn

As a cold new world before me is born

Let me glide with the porpoise

Under the bows of swift liners

And ponder the ancient purpose

Amidst the bones of ancient mariners

Let me stifle the Kraken

May he envious burn

As I at last the ancient purpose learn

Never to utter

Pen to spurn

And let me bathe in wonder

As I spiral down the emerald vortex

Never as a mortal to return

Señoritas De Consuelo

My third lady is the surf

She has much to teach

My second lady is the moon

She's always out of reach

My first is like the living white line

That follows me as I walk along the beach

She's sometimes near and sometimes gone

With silken hair and eyes like fawns

And purest skin to write upon

How do I sip this fair one's tea

Without the others close by

And permission from the sea?

Real or dream, I don't yet know

What lies beneath her haunting glow?

Salty tear or sugar kiss?

Darkest pain or brightest bliss?

Priceless pearls or shards of shell?

I wish not, but know too well

Only time will tell

Coconut Head

Locked away in the annuls of history

There lies a secret enshrouded in mystery

An endless riddle forever unsolved

And a horrible death to all those involved

Those who seek the answer to this

Are thrown into an endless abyss

If you listen very close on a night very clear

Without loss of faith and lacking in fear

You can hear the faint echo of the voices of the dead

"What became of the coconut head"?

Legend tells of an ancient being

Not really a man

Not really a thing

A tropical boy once climbed a tree

So high his eyes for miles could see

He was after the coconut milk so sweet

And the crunchy delicious white coconut meat

When he reached out to grab this life-giving jewel

It opened its eyes and cried, "You are a fool!"

The boy fell to earth and at once was dead

Then fell the mysterious coconut head

It rolled like a bowling ball into the ocean

And swam like a fish with a circular motion

It beached upon the Farallon shoals

And decided there to start stealing souls

From that day hence to the day this was written

Each man who saw this being was smitten

And all who seek it end up dead

Such is the legend of the coconut head

Freedom

Fly from me

Oh spirit of weight

Loose my chains of tame restraint

The cold will chill my bones

My limbs will twitch and shiver

My heart will hum its race

In the clear night breeze

Under the piercing crescent moon

Leaning on the post of the pier

Watch my breath seek the backlit sky

Numb water numbs my boots

Heels sink into shifting sand

Totter, reach, catch and hold

Oiled, splintery wood

Unplug feet and walk

Away from light

From man-made light

Into the night

After the live white line

Which leads on

And on

Seadream

Slowly and painfully

The cold water sinks its fangs

Into my bones

I feel every wound

I've ever had

Slowly and quietly

The venom numbs the pain

And seeks my heart

My breaths are short and shallow

Between gulps of the salty ocean

Faces flash before the eye

Of my mind

Love is a childhood memory

I can only feel my heart

Pounding thick, cold blood

Into the salty, deep ocean

Fear grips me

Stars above me

Monsters below me

What have I done?

A hideous smile leaps upon my face

With all my strength I yell "Concomitanta!"

And break into maniacal laughter

And then into violent weeping

What have I done?

What have I failed to do?

How many have I hurt?

And how badly?

I start to swim

To what looks like the shore

And I know I won't hurt them anymore

And I will not spurn love

Or make them sad

And I see a huge fin

Flash in front of my face

A few feet away

And another beside me just as close

And I swim with all my might

But I'm numb

And not going anywhere

I see a fin coming towards me

And strike with what strength

I have left

But the blow is not felt

And I awake in a puddle of sweat

Feeling like I'm going to hell

And like I've killed someone

And someone knows

And they're coming for me

They're going to expose me

And all the horrible things I've done

It was only a dream

But what have I done?

Goodnight

Tying the TV antenna to the cross trees

Half way up the mast

Arms wrapped around steel steps

And bars around the mast

I thought a wonderful thought

Words raced into my head

'I am the Indian!'

Tears began to trickle

Then stream

For at once I had awakened

Into my fondest dream

Moon rested very quietly

Just above the water

A very faint, sleepy orange

A sliver

It was a sliver, a perfect arc

Lying in the lower quadrants like a bowl

But look closely

I can see an almost indistinguishable enclosed circle

Of charcoal sky

By the same orange color

By this point in my writing

The moon has retired

Into the sea

Another dragger leads on one side

Close enough to see the cabin and gear clearly

Under its bright mast lights

Just below Mendocino

It's a pretty sight from the water at night

I can still see the smoke of home

Above the mill lights

And I can see lightning above it

The stars are out above us

Beautiful and bright

We're running down the hill

To Bodega Head for Dover

And off Tomales for English

Where we hope to run out of ice

It's evening

It's getting chilly on the flying bridge

Two hours to Arena

Nine to the lower end

Sleep nice

This poem is called

Good Night

The Salt Stream

One quiet, lonely Swan rests calmly on a dark
   mountain pond
The sky is alive with countless stars
And the air sparkles with glitter like a Christmas
   water toy
Tiny silver bells chime faintly in the tall pines
Which almost enclose the enchanted scene
There is no breeze
The water is still
The lovely bird is motionless
She seems suspended in midnight
For behind her there are no trees
There is no horizon
The water and sky melt together to form
An endless starlit expanse

Ever so slowly she bows her head

And whispers a song of distant Love

She wonders how she could be so alone

For the only reflections she sees are her own

And those of the stars

So distant above

One tiny glowing tear

Rolls down her trembling cheek

In slow motion it falls

And shatters the dark still pond

Into a pink morning sky that startles and stings

The Eagle's waking eye

His racing heart pounds

A symphony of distant love

And his gaze turns upward in the midst of sorrow's pain

For he's not yet sure if the stream down his face is tears

Or if it's rain

Laser

Hurting kind

Once more blind

Shocks of youth

From the wire I grip

With hearts below

Sporting thorns I've thrust

Awaiting my fall

Eyes of green

And gray of Mother's fury

And peace of Mother's breast

Burn longing and fear

Through the shallow pool

To the rocky bed

Of my stagnant soul

Why such fear

My love?

My love

Or my dream?

A crumb for a starving wretch

Or a feast for a patient king?

I should not fear

The fate that those I've passed

Would wish me

I will not fear

The storms of past or present

Behind those eyes

I shall ride the tempest

Of the storms to come

And shall be a lightning rod

For every bolt of life

Those gray clouds

Thrust into my newborn soul

Flooded

Mind not flooded with more than thoughts

Eyes flooded with more than blue

And albatross

Eyes not flooded with tears

But only blue, albatross

And visene

Heart not flooded with fears

But only calm, numb

And serene

Yesterday calls all day long

My answering machine is full

Tomorrow has quit trying

She knows I won't pick up

The mussels in the tide pools

Are all I care about right now

They can talk until the tide shuts them up

Who will they introduce me to one of these days?

Until then they will remain my only true friends

The tide is jealous

I must be going again

Tomorrow I'll be back

But will have forgotten today's talks

The mussels don't mind

They've told me the same stories

Every day

For a year

Westport Wind

Driving in the Westport Wind

On the Westport bluffs

At night

In the afterglow of sacrament

A head pounded by Grateful Dead

A heart pounding with freedom's bliss

In boundless decadence

I think

Driving down main street Westport

In the Westport rain

At night

Cottage blinds are drawn and dark

Not a soul in sight

But who can see souls?

Side by side the spirits are lined

On the edge of seaside cliffs

Not fifty yards away

To the hidden roar below

I listen

Westport in my southern glance

Vision nicked by Westport rain

Pickup tilted by Westport Wind

In delicious, warm content

I grin

Sailors' Eyes

Leaves in fall

And breakers' eyes

From the deep the call

Of evening skies

The depth is all

A sensuous surprise

To heed this call

With maddened cries

I set my course

For evening skies

I point my bow

Toward evening skies

Seas of pink and azure west

The moon and stars begin to rise

From their sleep and quiet rest

To their glory in evening skies

Seconds from her farewell kiss

She bows her head and blinks her eyes

The blessed moon in utter bliss

Says goodnight to sailors' eyes

Seconds from her parting glance

I kneel alone at starboard gunwale

Held by love's enchanting trance

My vision bound in a misty tunnel

A faint, ghostly orange thread

Through my sleepy, boyish eyes

Weaves its way into my head

Surrounded by a canvas black

And filled with misty gray

Stirs the pool of this sailor's romance

And nearly puts me on my back

I dread to see another day

As I fall into her silken hands

I turn for a moment to the sea

So gently angry and deep

She fills my yearning heart with bliss

And whispers secrets just for me

I turn back to find the moon has gone to sleep

I smile and blow her a kiss

Growing Pains

A Man Now

Walking through a stubble field of corn

A man now

I picture a story book, tattered and worn

And wonder how time slipped by so unnoticed

One minute I'm killing wasps

In the eaves of our house

With my brother

The next I'm a thousand miles from home

Trying to pay bills and finish school

I can see in the distance a nice new home

Built right where our old farm house used to stand

And another one where our barn was

And where our chicken shed once stood

An empty swimming pool

Houses, houses everywhere

There used to be only plum bushes, sage brush

And space where we lived

Not even a paved lane from the highway

There stands a house right over the spot

Where I learned not to finish off a jack rabbit

With a .410 from two inches away

I remember that day

Coming home covered with warm blood

And rabbit brains

I don't see my brother much any more

Or my sister or my parents

Only people who don't know me

Come to think of it

No one really knows me now

Not even me

To Be or Not to Be

To be or not to be...

That is not the question

Perhaps who to be, or

Who not to be

Who to be...

Who to be...

Who to be when who I am

Or who I'd like to be is

Afraid to be because of what

Who I am thinks others want

Me to be

Who gives a damn who

Others want me to be?

Maybe I shouldn't

But I do

Or maybe why to be

Is the question

The unfortunate, and sometimes

The fortunate, who aren't blinded

By their fortune

Wonder why to be

Most often the desperate

Wonder why to be when

They've given up on who they are

I've wondered why – to be

Or not to be

Who am I?

Why?

The Brook

A flash of warm, delicious brown catches little Hans'
 eye
"A fish!" cries he, "A fish!"
"It's not a silver salmon, the color of the sky
Racing to her home in the sea, that cold, deep sea."

Silence and stealth are shattered like glass
As the boy races through the tall reeds and grass
To capture this leaf fallen from a red oak
At the edge of the brook the mud cakes his ass
"I almost was lost in the gurgly torrent of this
 mighty wild brook as I lost my footing on its
 treacherous edge."
"It's a leaf! A boring maple leaf. Just a boring old,
 stupid old, dummy maple leaf!"

This leaf disappeared under a log in the flow

And Hans scampered home through the cottonwood snow.

Sometime later this brown maple red oak fish
    emerged from the turbulent darkness
Not to be swept away down the gurgly torrent
But to be lazily, contemplatively ambled off into a
    channel
A very slow, placid channel off in the trees
This channel did turn to virtual marsh
And reeds stopped the leaf to virtual still

The mainstream of time forgets song and rhyme
While quiet marsh pools are gardens sublime of
    sights unfelt

And feelings unseen
Colored like dreams, in time they do melt

The next time Hans approached the brook
The oak had gained much weight
He had moved away shortly after that day
And had returned late in life by fate
The cottonwoods were bent and weathered
Little Hans had grown up
And his dreams were bent and tethered
And the marsh had long since dried up

Lost

My life has taken a treacherous turn

Over a bridge I am watching burn

I see myself on the other side

Of a bottomless crevasse

So what am I doing here? Alas!

Along with myself I left behind

A suitcase of dreams and a forgotten past

I no longer see a goal

And as I gaze into that horrible hole

I spit reality into that foul mist

And lost is the need to learn

That I have reached the point

Of no return

Memories

With numbered days I watch the sun retire

Into the forgiving sea

She embraces me and massages my troubled soul

As the distant sky turns to fire

Even in a setting so utterly serene

They hunt me like a lioness

A familiar feeling brings them back

But the usual pain is not as cruel

Fallen asleep are my lesser fears

And the water on my cheeks is no longer tears - it's visene

A dinosaur is my happiness

And lives only in green fields of stone

But as a groaning vessel returns to port

I must return from my resort

And back to life I must report

Sails fall limp and lifeless

And I am still alone

Soon dinosaurs will be places to run

And as their vortices emerge

I can feel the bagpipes' opium dirge

And the setting of the sun

Broken Anchor

A thousand wings could not assume

This broken anchor mired

Severed from its tether chain

By countless nicks in its strongest link

Plunging down the lightless drink

Its maiden ship never again to groom

This sleeping anchor mired

Buried deep in finest silt

Held in place by weightless cord

Waiting for its schwartzes mord

Its barren path to never resume

This frozen anchor mired

Left to rust away in silence

Seldom noticed in useful years

Now inspires not a single tear

Resting in its matron's womb

This forgotten anchor mired

I wished it to be a playhouse

Full of laughter and innocent smiles

Every room unlocked if not open

And purged of air unpleasant

A home for one divine companion

With couches touched by none before

And a virgin surprise behind every door

But my heart lies silent forevermore

Torn by love's uncivil war

On the dark, forsaken ocean floor

This broken anchor mired

Cat in Cage

Cat in cage evokes

Slow, slow adrenaline

Quiet, peaceful explosion

Tight, high-pitched tension

A frog on the edge of a leap

A split second after a quiet

Still night is violated by a sudden

Crash in the brush a few feet away

Fear, anger, nervousness from the void

Flow in granite veins

Gripping in terror

To their life's blood

Which has suddenly become frozen -

- Poison

Junk House Blues

I woke up this morning
      with my head in a bass drum
I can't feel my hands
      and my throat is still numb
Another shot of whiskey
      and my heart will mellow out
Maintaining the perfect balance
      That's what it's all about

There's a body in one corner
      and another in the other
I think that one is Uncle
      The other is my brother
Last night was sort of bleary, sort of eerie,
      sort of great
Last night was four days long
      by my watch's calendar date

I drag my humming body upstairs
      and turn on the cartoons
I plop down in the chair
      by the table of bottles and spoons
A brush against the window
      It's just a branch, I'm certain
I slowly cross the creaky floor
      and peek behind the curtain

It's snowing in the city
      and the scene is enchanted and charmed
It's really quite a pity
      the snow blower bruises on my arms
And there's only one sure way to thaw
      my hollow, frozen head
Scoop some drifts up with a straw
      and try to go back to bed

I know it will never happen
      if I lift that hollow pin
I know I won't be nappin'
      for another four day spin
But lo and behold it all must end
      and the end is near I fear
We're running short on money to spend
      and the sky is getting clear

Bye

The time has come to say goodbye

To all that I hold dear

To spread these fettered wings and fly

Though I do not know to where

Fleeting wisdom I have spurned

And I'm sad to say I fear

That long ago my heart did die

And it's time for the rest to burn

Farewell, true friends

Farewell, dear God

Farewell to all the rest

Farewell good roads my steps have crossed

You know it's for the best

But the incessant pain

Of acid rain

In my wretched shrinking veins

Does knock again

On the door of my dimly lit den

I must drop my shrinking pen

I long for you, oh sacred dream

I will turn to the ocean blue

When through the mystic veil I pass

At last I will find you

King Arthur

Mordred was the son of a king

But he wore no royal signet ring

He plotted to lay his father low

With just one lightning fateful blow

He carried high his ornate lance

And threw about his hateful glance

The king grew weary of his son's disgrace

And had left the fight to put him in his place

He waited for that dreaded day

He would face his son with nothing to say

He did not know how it all went wrong

Or from whence came the dirge

Where there once was a song

Nor did Mordred perceive the true enemy's snare

And to numb the pain did his best not to care

He thought, 'What kind of king

Would bear with pride his royal crest

And not hail his own who for a time did his best'?

The king drew the bridge

When the boy would not agree

And would not let it down

When the man still could not see

His way as the only true answer in life

They grew distant and spoke not

To keep still the strife

But the ending to the legend today is not true

For I, dear father, do not wish to slay you

I ask your forgiveness

And I long for your pride

And when you fail in your age

I want to be by your side

I love you, King Arthur

Though I can't call you king

Please understand, I can't wear your thoughts

But I'll proudly wear your ring

And you must believe I care how you are

Though from you for so long I have been so very far

I care where you're going

And how fares your inner man

And if you are walking in the way of the master plan

If I never convince you in any other way

You'll hear the thunder of hoofs in the distance someday

I'll vault with my lance over that ominous moat

And the sword of the Spirit

We'll hold at each other's throats

I used to run

But have never been able to hide

So many times I've cut my throat swelled with pride

"Choose you this day whom you will serve!"

God's surgical steel in our hands will not swerve

And you can say, "Follow me son, we will serve the King."

And peace and great joy

Throughout the kingdom will ring

Like the unclean spirit

The bridge is dropped with a word

From the Son of the King

Whose light our earthly vision has blurred

And we will walk side by side through the kingdom someday

If we but embrace from our hearts

Kneel

And pray

The River

Life starts with a rush of cold and blinding light
Like a waterfall on a sunny winter day
We're hurled into the river
Good parents scoop their young up out of the current
And set them in their canoe
Others turn away as the newborn is tossed about
Either drowned or beaten into something less than human
The canoe is guided by father at the stern
But made swift and stable by mother's effort at the bow
As the two cooperate, the craft glides peacefully
Through any danger, twist, or turn
Working together, they navigate the channels
If either quits, they are pushed to the bank

If they trade places, the canoe spins out of control

And they wrap around a rock

The stern must listen to the bow

Dangers lie just below the surface

Which can only be seen by mother

The bow must listen to the stern

The mission and course are set from above

And father is the pilot, charts written on his heart

As long as the Chart Maker is living there

And baby sits safe and dry in between

Watching and learning from both

Safe from what lies beneath

Or what lurks on the shores

And longs to know the Chart Maker

Like mother and father do

And have her own canoe some day

About the Author

John Oswald was born and grew up in Nebraska, USA. Music, art, and writing came naturally at an early age. He is the author of a successful how-to book, The Complete Debt Relief Manual.

His family vacationed in Fort Bragg, California when he was 10. He contracted sea sickness. Not the kind where you throw up on a boat, the kind that made him sick to leave and go back to "the rug" as his California cousins dubbed the Midwest. John's family returned to Fort Bragg for another visit when he was 12.

At age 20, after a failed first attempt at college, he joined the Navy. His passion for creative writing awakened at that time.

After leaving the Navy due to a near-fatal car accident, John became deeply disillusioned with religion and relationships. He moved to Fort Bragg, California in 1988, where he worked as a deck hand on a fishing boat and fell madly in love with the sea. He had found paradise in Mendocino County. His writing became an obsession. But the call of stability and practicality drowned out the call of the sea and the dream of writing as a profession, and he moved back to Nebraska and finished his bachelor's degree in Mechanical Engineering.

As an engineer, he has had the opportunity to learn and master technical writing, which isn't his first love, but it has been paying the bills.

John currently lives and works as a professional procedure writer in the United Arab Emirates and is married to his best friend and muse, Luisa. He continues to write poetry and work on a collection of short stories and the draft of his first novel. The sea still calls to him.

John would love to hear from you. Email him at: quetzal63@gmail.com.

www.ingramcontent.com/pod-product-compliance
Lightning Source LLC
LaVergne TN
LVHW092322080426
835508LV00040B/1102